Peter J. Gabbiness?   Queen H...

GW00838662

COMPUTER MONOGRAPHS

General Editor: Stanley Gill, M.A., Ph.D., *Professor of Computing Science, Imperial College, London*

Associate Editor: J. J. Florentin, Ph.D., *Imperial College, London*

I

LIST PROCESSING

LIST PROCESSING

J. M. FOSTER

Senior Research Fellow
Department of Engineering
Aberdeen University

MACDONALD : LONDON

AND

AMERICAN ELSEVIER INC: NEW YORK

© J. M. Foster 1967

First Published 1967
Second impression 1968
Third impression 1968
Fourth impression 1969
First published in paperback 1969

Sole distributors for the United States and Dependencies
American Elsevier Publishing Company, Inc.
52 Vanderbilt Avenue
New York, N.Y. 10017

Sole distributors for the British Isles and Commonwealth
Macdonald & Co. (Publishers) Ltd
P.O. Box 2 L.G.
49–50 Poland Street
London W.1

All remaining areas
Elsevier Publishing Company
P.O. Box 211
Jan van Galenstraat 335
Amsterdam
The Netherlands

Library of Congress Catalog Card Number 68-9207

British Standard Book Numbers
SBN 356 02225 0   Cloth bound edition
SBN 356 02994 8   Paper bound edition

PRINTED IN GREAT BRITAIN

CONTENTS

1. Introduction   1
   Origins of List Processing   2

2. The Representation of Lists   4
   Lists in the Computer   4
   Lists on Paper   7
   Simple List Operations   9

3. Operations on Lists   13
   Recursion   14
   The Efficiency of Recursion   17
   Push-down Lists   19
   Operations that alter Lists   20

4. More Advanced Features   22
   Atoms   24
   Vectors   24
   Circular Lists   26
   Lists on Auxiliary Storage   27

5. An Example of List Processing   29

6. Garbage Collection   33
   Declaration of wanted Lists   35
   Declaration of unwanted Lists   39
   Garbage Collection and Vectors   40

7. Some Typical List Languages   41
   IPL-V   42
   LISP   44
   SLIP   47
   FLPL   48
   COMIT   48

8. The Future of List Processing   51

References   53

I

INTRODUCTION

The computer's *forte* is arithmetic. Simple numerical programs can easily be made out of the machine orders that add, subtract, multiply or divide. But finding the numbers can be difficult. The computer's store of data is organized in a particular way. If the information needed in a program can be arranged so that it is visited in an order which conforms with the structure of the store, then all is well. Each word in the store is numbered, and it is by referring to this number (the address of the word) that the contents of the word can be used or changed. The machine can compute numbers, so the data must be arranged to make the computation of successive addresses easy. When the order in which the words have to be used is complicated, the finding of the addresses may be a major part of the program.

If a computer is to translate from Russian into English, control a set of traffic lights, prove theorems or make school time-tables it has to manipulate data with complex inter-relationships. These relationships may mean that the words in the store have to be visited in intricate and elaborate patterns. List processing is concerned with a kind of modelling of objects inside the computer which expressly shows their relationships, in a way which makes finding their addresses easy. The name 'list processing' indicates that the basis of the ideas lies in ordered sets. If a group of items needs visiting in a particular order it can be made into an ordered set. An item may be in several ordered sets. Many examples may be given. A queue is an ordered set of entries; a sentence is an ordered set of words; a matrix is an ordered set of vectors, each of which is an ordered set of numbers; a program is an ordered set of operations; a firm's employees have an ordered set of names and its stock catalogue contains an ordered set of items. In other examples the order within the set may be unimportant. A drawing is a collection of lines, an electrical circuit is a collection of sets of connections and a railway system is a set of tracks which join members of a set of stations. This idea of sets is so fundamental that the techniques used have been part of programming from the earliest times. List processing is not a new method: it is a system of practices which are widely current.

The primitive operations that are wanted for manipulating lists are not the same as those for arithmetic. Suppose that a railway system is to be represented in the computer by a set of station names, each of which is associated with a list of stations directly connected to it and some information about the connections. The sort of operation that is likely to be useful is 'where (in the store) is the name of the next station' or 'add another number to this list' or 'what is the first item in this list'. Although these operations could be written by the programmer in terms of the operations of the machine, and in the running program they will be so represented, list programming is usually done through a compiler; the programmer writes in a language in which it is easy to express the thing he wants to do, and the compiler program translates this into machine code which can be obeyed by the computer.

We shall be concerned with languages which are explicitly for list processing, that is, they contain primitive operations for manipulating lists: we shall not much consider languages which work by doing list processing but conceal the simple operations from the user, who may think that he is working directly in terms of, say, sentences. This is not because of any superiority of the former, but simply because the list processing primitives and their implementation are the primary concern of this book. The list programming primitives are in a way the machine orders of list processing and using them has some of the advantages and disadvantages of using machine code.

Languages for list processing have arisen in two ways. Either they have been languages explicitly intended for lists, and they include ways of doing numerical work with more or less convenience; or they have been adaptations of languages originally developed for numerical work on to which the list processing operations have been grafted. The latter offer the advantage that they are widely understood and that a great range of numerical programs is already available in them. Programs often involve both numerical work and list processing so that the advantage of access to a library of existing routines can be considerable. On the other hand the special list processing languages may be more convenient to use. In this book we shall express programs for operating on lists in ALGOL (with some modifications) except where other list processing languages are being discussed. This is in order to take advantage of the common understanding of ALGOL.

Origins of List Processing

List processing starts to be important when the simplest methods of using the store break down. In simple programs the computer store is often arranged in separate sections representing separate things: vectors, matrices, decoding tables, strings of characters and the like. The sizes of these blocks of data are known beforehand and the addresses in the computer are allocated to them before work starts.

2

This is often satisfactory, but difficulties arise. A common example is the need to read into the store a set of numbers when the size of the set is not known until the reading is finished. How much store should be laid aside for this vector and what should be done if there are several of them? The techniques of list processing grew from solutions to this sort of problem, which occurs even more often in real-time and non-numerical work where the needs of the program for data space may be unknown until it is in the course of running. But list processing is more than a flexible method of using the store. It happens that the methods used for storage allocation can give the store a complicated structure, and so the same devices provide the programmer with a solution to the problem of manipulating and representing data with structure. It is worth bearing in mind that these two rather separate uses do exist, and influence the approach of programmers to different extents according to their needs.

Early list processing languages were invented in order to carry out specific projects of a non-numerical nature. The sequence of languages called IPL (21, 22, 26) started out in order to provide satisfactory methods of organizing information for work in theorem proving and problem solving, a field in which the amount of storage needed is very variable and unpredictable, and in which the structure of the lists carries important information. LISP (16, 17, 18) was developed partly for the use of a project called the 'Advice Taker' which was intended to operate in a complex way on English statements about situations. A language called FLPL (11) which was embedded in FORTRAN was produced to write programs for proving theorems in geometry. COMIT (7, 31) was devised for language research.

In all these cases the stimulus of a particular need for complex organization of data led to languages which were found useful for many purposes. It is not the purpose of this book to give a detailed account of any of the important list languages. Such accounts are available in the literature and especially in the programming manuals of the languages. Instead, a discussion will be given of the principles involved and some of the common methods used to implement the languages, in order to try to extract the general techniques from the particular environments in which they are found.

3

2

THE REPRESENTATION OF LISTS

The objects and relationships which are being operated on in list processing are represented at two levels. The computer represents lists by the contents of its stores, but the programmer represents them by marks on paper. The programmer's notation may be a complete description of the contents of the store or it may express just those features which seem to be relevant. In this chapter we shall describe the simpler features of the computer's representation and notations for use by the programmer on paper.

Lists in the Computer

Consider a program which is intended to read in a sentence, then to arrange the words in alphabetical order and finally to print them out in this order. If we suppose that the words when they have been read are packed as closely as possible in the store at, say, six characters to the word, then the sentence might be represented thus.

```
100    C  O  L  D  + I
101    S  +  D  E  L  E
102    T  E  R  I  O  U
103    S  +  T  O  + T
104    H  E  +  M  A  Y
105    O  N  N  A  I  S
106    E  + ── ── ── ──
```

The letters will be represented by small integers packed into the words which have the addresses given on the left. The spaces between words are indicated by the plus sign. When these words have been arranged in dictionary order they will appear like this.

```
200    C  O  L  D  + D
201    E  L  E  T  E  R
202    I  O  U  S  + I
203    S  +  M  A  Y  O
204    N  N  A  I  S  E
205    +  T  H  E  + T
206    O  + ── ── ── ──
```

4

Clearly, though this is not a difficult piece of programming, it is unnecessarily awkward. It would be much easier to pack the characters less closely and start each word of the sentence at a new address. The ordered form is then much easier to obtain because the quantities to be moved are now multiples of a single computer word instead of being split up among the words.

100	C O L D + —
101	I S + — — —
102	D E L E T E
103	R I O U S +
104	T O + — — —
105	T H E + — —
106	M A Y O N N
107	A I S E + —

This can be rearranged to give the following stores.

200	C O L D + —
201	D E L E T E
202	R I O U S +
203	I S + — — —
204	M A Y O N N
205	A I S E + —
206	T H E + — —
207	T O + — — —

The programming can be made easier by adding to the representation of the sentence a vector giving the address of the start of each word of the sentence.

300	100		100	C O L D + —
301	101		101	I S + — — —
302	102		102	D E L E T E
303	104		103	R I O U S +
304	105		104	T O + — — —
305	106		105	T H E + — —
			106	M A Y O N N
			107	A I S E + —

We can now derive a similar vector of addresses which gives the address of the start of each word in alphabetical order, without moving any of the packed words at all.

400	100
401	102
402	101
403	106
404	105
405	104

5

This piece of programming is fairly easy. Clearly there could be many vectors of addresses representing the words of the sentence in various orders without affecting the stores containing the characters, and new words could be added to the system without disturbing those already there or the vectors already in existence. The important feature of this rather trivial example is that it may be an advantage to manipulate the addresses of quantities rather than the quantities themselves, both for ease of programming and for economy of store. This is a commonplace of programming which is a fundamental basis of list processing.

Another simple example of the use of calculation with addresses comes from matrices. Consider a two-dimensional matrix held in the store and a vector giving the starting address for each of the rows. Suppose that this matrix is being used in the solution of simultaneous equations in which it is useful to choose the largest pivot element at each stage in the eliminations in order to conserve accuracy. The consequent interchange of rows which is necessary can be achieved by interchanging the elements of the vector of addresses instead of the whole rows, if the gain in speed from not moving the numbers compensates the loss from referring to them indirectly.

A second technique which forms a basic part of list processing is the use of a chain of items, linked by making each item contain the address of the next item on the chain. Consider again the representation of a sentence in the computer store, this time in yet another way. The words will be packed, but each computer store will contain the address of the store which holds the next part of the sentence

100	T	H	E	101
101	D	O	G	102
102	B	I	T	103
103	T	H	E	104
104	M	A	N	0

The column of numbers on the left are the store addresses, the numbers on the right are part of the contents of the store. They give the address of the next store in the sentence. The zero indicates that there is no following element. If words have to be added to this sentence or deleted from it this can be done without moving the existing words, since the sequence of stores in which they occur has no significance.

100	T	H	E	105
101	D	O	G	102
102	B	I	T	103
103	T	H	E	106
104	M	A	N	0
105	M	A	D	101
106	F	A	T	104

Clearly a chain is an ordered set of items.

The third and final step towards list processing is to realize that the items in a chain could be addresses, either of things like the groups of letters which have been used as an example, or of the starts of more chains of the same kind.

100	R O B I N S	200	100,201
101	O N + — — —	201	103,0
102	J O H N + —	202	204,203
103	S M I T H +	203	206,0
104	J O E + — —	204	100,205
		205	102,0
		206	103,207
		207	104,0

In the stores shown on the right there is a chain starting at address 200 and consisting of two items, a pointer to the word ROBINSON and another to the word SMITH: starting at 202 is a chain containing two items, the first being a chain holding ROBINSON and JOHN, the second a chain holding SMITH and JOE. We shall drop the term 'chain' for general use and refer to 'lists'.

It would seem to be unnecessary to maintain the distinction between the two addresses in each store, but it is found in practice to be a useful one and we will continue to make the first pointer refer to the elements in a list and the second to show the next list store.

The data for a list processing problem inside the computer normally consists of two parts. There are stores containing the objects which are being manipulated, like the words in a sentence, which are not moved about; and there are the list stores which contain addresses pointing to other lists or to the objects.

The objects which do not have the two pointer nature will be called atoms, since they are indivisible. We shall not discuss the actual forms of atoms much in what follows, though a list processing scheme will certainly have standard sorts of atoms to represent standard objects. The examples with which we shall be concerned in this book tend to be about operations like 'reverse the order of the items in the list' rather than operations on the contents of lists like 'print the name of the first man in this list'. This is because we are interested in manipulating lists rather than in particular representations of particular jobs.

Lists on paper

The notation for lists which has been used so far expresses exactly the contents of the computer, but it is quite impossibly cumbersome for use as a paper notation. Since we are not interested in the actual stores which contain the information, the addresses can be dropped and the stores represented by boxes containing two parts, out of which come pointers to the boxes referred to. Once again the right-hand pointer will connect the list stores and the left-hand pointer will indicate the item. The notation for atoms will be arbitrary. The following is the representation of the list which started at address 200 in the previous example.

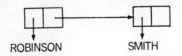

ROBINSON   SMITH

The list starting at 202 is

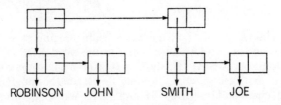

ROBINSON   JOHN   SMITH   JOE

This notation shows all the information which is normally relevant but it is still over-elaborate in many cases.

A notation which is simpler for the user can be devised in which the elements of a list are grouped together in brackets and separated by commas.

((ROBINSON,JOHN),(SMITH,JOE))

This is much more like an intuitive notation for lists. Notice that in the sentence

(COLD,IS,DELETERIOUS,TO,THE,MAYONNAISE)

the left pointer of the first cell points to

COLD

and the right pointer to

(IS,DELETERIOUS,TO,THE,MAYONNAISE)

This notation will be used throughout the book when it contains sufficient information, and the notation with boxes will be used when the need for greater accuracy about the contents of the machine arises. The sort of situation where the simple bracket notation is not enough can be seen from this example.

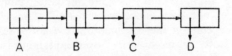

A   B   C   D

8

The list which starts with the first word is

$$(A,B,C,D)$$

and the list starting at the second word is

$$(B,C,D)$$

The bracket expressions do not show the fact that the two lists consist in part of the same stores of the computer, so that if one of the lists is altered the other will also be altered without any explicit reference being made to it. The same bracket expression covers the case when the lists consist of different stores in the computer and an alteration to one leaves the other unaffected.

Simple List Operations

We can now consider some elementary operations on lists and a program made out of them. The first that we shall introduce are the pair $hd(x)$ and $tl(x)$, standing for the head of x and the tail of x, which give as their values the left and right pointers of x. If l is the list

$$(COLD,IS,DELETERIOUS,TO,THE,MAYONNAISE)$$

then $hd(l)$ is

$$COLD$$

and $tl\ (l)$ is

$$(IS,DELETERIOUS,TO,THE,MAYONNAISE)$$

and if n is the list

$$((ROBINSON,JOHN),(SMITH,JOE))$$

then $hd(n)$ is

$$(ROBINSON,JOHN)$$

and $tl(n)$ is

$$((SMITH,JOE))$$

The precise effect of the operators on these lists is worthy of consideration. If reference is made to the representations of them which show the addresses, it can be seen how the unsymmetrical effect arises. By convention we shall say that the tl of a list of one item is zero.

$$m = (SMITH)$$
$$tl(m) = 0$$

9

The operators are undefined on atomic objects. Compounding is allowed, for example if *p* is

$$(ROBINSON,JOHN)$$

$$
\begin{aligned}
hd(p) &= ROBINSON \\
tl(p) &= (JOHN) \\
hd(tl(p)) &= JOHN \\
tl(tl(p)) &= 0
\end{aligned}
$$

and in the list *n*

$$((ROBINSON,JOHN),(SMITH,JOE))$$

$$hd(tl(hd(tl(n)))) = JOE$$

Note that successive elements of a list are given by

$$hd(x), hd(tl(x)), hd(tl(tl(x))), hd(tl(tl(tl(x)))) .....$$

The operations *hd* and *tl* dissect a list. To construct one the operator *cons* is used. If *x* is an atom or a list and *y* is a list, then *cons(x,y)* has as its value a new list cell whose left pointer indicates *x* and whose right pointer is *y*: that is, *cons(x,y)* is the list consisting of the item *x* in front of the existing list *y*. If *s* is

$$COLD$$

and *t* is

$$(IS,DELETERIOUS,TO,THE,MAYONNAISE)$$

then *cons(s,t)* is

$$(COLD,IS,DELETERIOUS,TO,THE,MAYONNAISE)$$

and if *u* is

$$(ROBINSON,JOHN)$$

and *v* is

$$((SMITH,JOE))$$

then *cons(u,v)* is

$$((ROBINSON,JOHN),(SMITH,JOE))$$

By convention we form a list of one element by making the second parameter of *cons* zero.

$$
\begin{aligned}
k &= SMITH \\
cons(k,0) &= (SMITH)
\end{aligned}
$$

Although it would be possible to allow the second parameter of *cons* to be an atom, we shall never do so but we shall preserve the convention that items of a list are shown by the left pointer (the first

10

parameter) and the right pointer (the second parameter) links the list stores.

Cons can be compounded.

$$h = \text{SMITH}$$
$$j = \text{JOE}$$
$$cons(cons(h,cons(j,0)),0) = ((\text{SMITH,JOE}))$$

The list consisting of

$$(a,b,c,d, \dots\dots z)$$

is formed by

$$cons(a,cons(b,cons(c,cons(d, \dots\dots cons(z,0))))) \dots)$$

Clearly *hd* and *tl* are the inverse operations to *cons* and in every respect the following are true

$$hd(cons(a,b)) = a$$
$$tl(cons(a,b)) = b$$

But the converse rules are not quite true. The value of

$$cons(hd(x),tl(x))$$

is a new cell in the computer store which contains the same pointers that the original cell *x* did: that is, it is a copy of the cell *x*, not the cell *x* itself.

These operations will enable us to write a short program to act on a list which is assumed to be in the computer. Suppose that we are given a list of pairs of surnames and Christian names, like

$$((\text{ROBINSON,JOHN}),(\text{SMITH,JOE}))$$

and we wish to obtain a list of the surnames only. The length of the list is unknown and it does not matter in which order the list of surnames appears. Let *l* contain the original list and the required list will be built up in *m*. The list *l* will be destroyed.

$$m := 0;$$
loop: **if** $l \neq 0$ **then**
    begin $m := cons(hd(hd(l)),m)$;
        $l := tl(l)$;
        goto *loop*
    end;

Consider this operating on the list above. At *loop* the first time

$$l = ((\text{ROBINSON,JOHN}),(\text{SMITH,JOE}))$$
$$m = 0$$

After obeying the compound statement and going again to *loop*

$$l = ((SMITH,JOE))$$
$$m = (ROBINSON)$$

and the third time *loop* is reached

$$l = 0$$
$$m = (SMITH,ROBINSON)$$

and the program stops. The order of the surnames is the reverse of that in the original list.

3

OPERATIONS ON LISTS

This chapter starts by discussing two methods of writing programs, recursion and iteration, using the operations which have been introduced, together with two new operations, *atom* and *eq*. The procedure *atom(x)* has the value true if x is an atom and is false otherwise. The procedure *eq(x,y)* has the value true if the two atoms, x and y, are identical and is false otherwise. It is only defined when the arguments are both atoms.

By iteration is meant the common way of programming, exemplified by the last program in the last chapter. Repeated operations are carried out by jumping back and going around a sequence of instructions until enough repetitions have been made. The following simple program is an iterative way of reversing the list l, putting the result into m.

```
       m := 0;
loop: if l ≠ 0 then
         begin m := cons(hd(l),m);
               l := tl(l);
               goto loop
         end;
```

The operation of this program is obvious from the example in the last chapter. Only the top level is reversed, so if the program is applied to

((ROBINSON,JOHN),(SMITH,JOE))

the result is

((SMITH,JOE),(ROBINSON,JOHN))

The next program puts into m the first atom which occurs in the list l, regardless of brackets.

```
loop: if atom(l) then m := l
      else
      begin l := hd(l);
            goto loop
      end;
```

13

The list *l* might take successively the values

((ROBINSON,JOHN),(SMITH,JOE))
(ROBINSON,JOHN)
ROBINSON

the last value being put into *m*.

Recursion

The previous programs are very simple ones which either go steadily down the tail pointers of a list or go down the head pointers. It often happens when going down the list that some operation has to be done on a sub-list, the main list being returned to when the sub-list has been processed. It may be the case that the work which has to be done on the sub-list is the same as, or a modified version of, the work which is being done on the main list. When this is the case, recursion may be a useful way of programming.

Recursion means exactly the same as it does in ordinary mathematics: the following is a recursive definition because the value of *factorial* is found by applying *factorial* again.

integer procedure *factorial(n)* ; **integer** *n*;
factorial := **if** *n*=0 **then** 1 **else** *n* × *factorial(n–1)* ;

Consider again the problem of finding the first atom of a list, this time with a recursive program. If the list is an atom then it is itself the answer. Otherwise it is necessary to find the first atom of the sub-list which is at the head of this list. The function to be performed on the sub-list is exactly the same as that on the main list. A procedure can be declared, which we shall call *firstatom* (17), whose value will be the first atom of its parameter.

list procedure *firstatom(x)* ; **list** *x*;
firstatom := **if** *atom(x)* **then** *x* **else** *firstatom(hd(x))* ;

A recursive program can also be written to reverse the top level of a list.

list procedure *rev(x,y)* ; **list** *x,y*;
rev := **if** *x*=0 **then** *y* **else** *rev(tl(x), cons(hd(x),y))* ;

To reverse the list *l*, putting the result into *m*, we can say

$$m := rev(l,0) ;$$

Consider how this program operates on the list

(A,(B,C),D)

writing the values of the parameters at each time that *rev* is called.

14

1st parameter	2nd parameter
(A,(B,C),D)	0
((B,C),D)	(A)
(D)	((B,C),A)
0	(D,(B,C),A)

When the first parameter reaches the value zero, the value of the second parameter is given to the function *rev*, which is then left. Control returns to the point after the previous call of *rev*, which assigns the value thus found to the function *rev* at this level. This is then left, and the process continues until the initial call is left, still with the same value.

The next procedure, which is also recursive, will look at all the atoms in a list to see whether any of them is equal to a given atom, no matter what structure the list has. Once again the process to be carried out on any sub-lists that there may be is identical with the process being carried out on the main list.

> **boolean procedure** *mem(a,l)* ; **list** *a,l* ;
> *mem* := **if** *atom(l)* **then** *eq(a,l)*
>   **else if** *mem(a,hd(l))* **then** true **else** *mem(a,tl(l))* ;

If the list is an atom then it can immediately be tested to see whether it is equal to *a*. Otherwise the same process is applied to the head. If this sub-list contains *a* then the answer is true and no more need be done. If the head does not contain *a* then the tail must be examined.

Writing recursive procedures is often unnatural until some practice has been obtained. It is common to think about the process on these lines. Suppose that the procedure *mem(a,l)* works for all lists included in *l*: then we can define it for *l* itself by the conditional expression

> **if** *mem(a,hd(l))* **then** true **else** *mem(a, tl(l))*

since *mem* works on both the head and the tail of *l*. This is satisfactory unless *l* is an atom, in which case it has no constituent lists, and the definition is *eq(a,l)*. Putting these together we obtain the procedure definition above.

These procedures are fairly straight-forward, but recursive programs can sometimes be decidedly complicated. The following program is not easy, though the same sort of argument will show how it works. Given a general list, *l*, make another list with the same atoms in the same order, but with the atoms all on the same level. Let *l* be

$$(A,(B,(C,D)),E)$$

Then the flattened version is

$$(A,B,C,D,E)$$

list procedure *flat(a,b)* ; **list** *a,b* ;
  flat := **if** *a*=0
    then *b*
    else if *atom(a)* **then** *cons(a,b)*
        else *flat(hd(a),flat(tl(a),b))* ;

The function *flat(a,b)* puts a flattened version of *a* in front of *b*. Hence *flat(l,0)* will be the required list. Suppose that *a* is a list and that *flat* works on all smaller lists, then

$$flat(tl(a),b)$$

will put a flattened version of *tl(a)* in front of *b*, and

$$flat(hd(a),flat(tl(a),b))$$

will put a flattened version of *hd(a)* in front of a flattened version of *tl(a)* in front of *b*; this is the correct definition. However, if *a* is empty the answer is *b*; and if *a* is an atom then *a* can be put immediately in front of *b* by *cons(a,b)*. Putting these three possibilities together gives the definition above. *Flat* operates on a list in the following manner.

  flat [(A,(B,(C,D)),E) , O]
  flat [A , *flat* [((B,(C,D)),E) , O]]
  flat [A , *flat* [(B,(C,D)) , *flat* [E , O]]]
  flat [A , *flat* [(B,(C,D)) , (E)]]
  flat [A , *flat* [B , *flat* [((C,D)) , (E)]]]
  flat [A , *flat* [B , *flat* [(C,D) , *flat* [(O , (E)]]]]
  flat [A , *flat* [B , *flat* [(C,D) , (E)]]]
  flat [A , *flat* [B , *flat* [C , *flat* [(D) , (E)]]]]
  flat [A , *flat* [B , *flat* [C , *flat* [D , *flat* [O , (E)]]]]]
  flat [A , *flat* [B , *flat* [C , *flat* [D , (E)]]]]
  flat [A , *flat* [B , *flat* [C , (D,E)]]]
  flat [A , *flat* [B , (C,D,E)]]
  flat [A , (B,C,D,E)]
  (A,B,C,D,E)

A very clear example of the reason for using recursion can be given using an arithmetic expression evaluator. Let the list *l* have one of the structures

$$(+,(a,b))   (-,(a,b))   (\times,(a,b))   (/,(a,b))$$

where *a* and *b* are either atoms with numerical values or lists of the same type of structure as *l*. A typical list is

$$(/,(+,(A,(-,(B,C)))),(\times,(/,(D,E)),F))$$

representing

$$(A+(B-C))/((D/E)\times F)$$

16

Recursion is used because, when an expression is being evaluated, the parameters must first be evaluated and then combined; and this evaluation is just the same as that on the upper level.

```
real procedure evaluate(l); list l;
begin list m,n;
    if atom(l) then evaluate := l
    else begin m := hd(hd(tl(l))); n := hd(tl(hd(tl(l))));
            evaluate := if hd(l)='+' then evaluate(m)+
                                                    evaluate(n)
                    else if hd(l)= '—' then evaluate(m)—
                                                    evaluate(n)
                    else if hd(l)= '×' then evaluate(m)
                                                ×evaluate(n)
                    else evaluate(m)/evaluate(n)
        end
end;
```

The Efficiency of Recursion

In some languages recursion is expensive in time or space or both. We shall consider where it is likely to be a better way of programming than iteration and shall show examples where it is wasteful and where it is efficient.

The danger and the power of recursion lie in the fact that, as ever deeper levels of calling are reached, the temporary storage and links must be preserved in order to have them available when control returns. If the recursion is very deep this may use a lot of store. If this record is valuable and will be used when the level is returned to then this may be satisfactory, but if it is not going to be used then it can be very wasteful indeed. Consider the recursive program which reverses a list.

```
list procedure rev(x,y); list x,y;
rev := if x=0 then y else rev(tl(x),cons(hd(x),y));
```

When this program is working the answer is being built up in the second parameter. When the first parameter is reduced to zero all the levels of recursion are left in turn without doing any work. If the list had contained a thousand sub-lists the procedure might have gone a thousand levels deep and then left these one by one without effect. This would be slow, and since each level of recursion might use a few stores of temporary memory the program might use without purpose several thousand stores. The iterative program for reversing the list uses no superfluous working space and does no redundant work. In this case the use of recursion could be enormously costly.

Similarly the recursive program for finding the first atom of a list was expensive compared with the iterative one. On the other hand, the recursive program for evaluating an expression was economical on these grounds. Consider the state when a list is to be evaluated that begins with plus. Then it is necessary to evaluate one parameter, remember it, evaluate the second parameter and then add the two numbers. This is precisely what the recursion does, and an attempt to do this without recursion may be cumbersome without being more efficient. The same is true of the procedure for flattening a list and for the one which finds whether an atom is a member of a list.

We can show this with a particularly elegant and simple example (29), a recursive program for copying a list. By a copy of a list is meant a list structure consisting of different cells in the computer store, but having the same relationships between its parts and pointing to the same atoms, If we say

$$m := l;$$

we have not made a copy of the list; m is the same list as l.

list procedure $copy(l)$; **list** l;
$copy := $ **if** $atom(l)$ **then** l **else** $cons(copy(hd(l)),copy(tl(l)))$;

Suppose that $copy$ works on all sub-lists of l. then

$$cons(copy(hd(l)),copy(tl(l)))$$

gives a new cell pointing to copies of the head and tail. If l is an atom then it is the value itself. The iterative program below, which puts a copy of b into l, is awkward and has no advantages.

```
l := b;
if atom(l) then goto exit;
p := m := q := 0;
r2 :if l = 0 then
begin rl :if p ≠ 0 then
        begin l := cons(hd(p),l) ; p := tl(p) ; goto rl end;
            if q = 0 then goto exit;
            p := cons(l,hd(q)) ;
            q := tl(q);
            l := hd(m);
            m := tl(m);
            goto r2
        end
end

else if atom(hd(l)) then
begin p := cons(hd(l),p) ;
        l := tl(l);
        goto r2
end
```

18

else
begin $m := cons(tl(l),m)$;
      $q := cons(p,q)$;
      $p := 0$;
      $l := hd(l)$;
      goto $r2$
end;

Of course, languages which have no recursion available provide other means of doing the same job, such as sets of procedures for sequencing through lists in various ways.

It may also be useful to avoid excessive depth of recursion arising from the tail of a list. The lack of symmetry between heads and tails means that the depth in terms of heads is often much less than that in terms of tails. It may be better to do recursion on the heads and iteration on the tails. The procedure below for $mem(a,l)$ may use less space than the fully recursive one.

boolean procedure $mem(a,l)$; **list** a,l;
n :**if** $atom(l)$ **then** $mem := eq(a,l)$
else if $mem(a,hd(l))$ **then** $mem :=$ **true**
else if $tl(l) = 0$ **then** $mem :=$ **false**
else begin $l := tl(l)$;
         goto n
    end;

Two rules to guide when recursion is useful are:
1. If it is easy to do iteratively, do so.
2. If the recursive version contains two calls of itself it may be useful.

Push-down Lists

Push-down lists are closely associated with recursion and list processing. A push-down list is a kind of queue in which the items to be processed first are those which were added last. It is also called a stack, a cellar and a last-in-first-out queue. The program which copied a list without the use of recursion operated with three push-down lists, p, q, and m. Another well-known use is in the evaluation of expressions in Reverse Polish Notation. This notation is particularly useful in computers because it avoids the use of brackets, and because of the simple way in which expressions can be evaluated. If an expression such as

$$a+b\times(c+d/e)/f$$

is rearranged in a functional notation with the function names placed after the arguments

$$(a,(b,(c,(d,e)/)+)\times,f)/)+$$

and the brackets and commas are left out

19

$$abcde/+\times f/+$$

the result is a Reverse Polish version of the original expression. It can be converted back into the bracketed form in an unique way because each of the operators has a known number of arguments. Proceeding from left to right through the Reverse Polish we can argue as follows. The *a* must be the argument of some operator; remember it. So must the *b*, *c*, *d* and *e*. The two arguments of divide must be the last two objects remembered, *d* and *e*, which may be combined, giving one number, the quotient, as result. Then the operator plus must have two arguments of which the first must be *c* and the second must be the quotient just found. By similar means we can find the structure of the whole expression. In order to evaluate such an expression held as a list, *l*, we can use the following program. It uses a push-down list to implement an algorithm which works in a very similar way to the above method of finding the arguments.

> *rep*:*t* := *hd(l)* ;
> *l* := *tl(l)* ;
> **if** *letter(t)* **then** *x* := *cons(t,x)*
> **else** *x* := *cons(apply(t,hd(x),hd(tl(x))),tl(tl(x)))* ;
> **goto** *rep* ;

The procedure called *apply* gives as its result the value of the operator, which is its first argument, applied to the parameters given in its second and third arguments. The push-down list, *x*, is added to when a variable is encountered or a partial result found, and items are taken off it to form the arguments of the arithmetic operators. These operations, of adding to push-down lists and taking items off them, are so frequent that some languages have special functions to do them.

Operations that alter Lists

So far the only functions that have been used are *cons, hd, tl, atom* and *eq*. These either examine an existing list or create a completely new one. They do not alter lists. The ability to change a list is both very powerful and very dangerous.

To change a list it is necessary to overwrite the whole of a cell or some part of one. We introduce three new operators, *set, sethd* and *settl*. The effect of *set(x,y)* is to overwrite the whole of the cell called *x* by the value of *y*. The effect of *sethd(x,y)* and *settl(x,y)* is to overwrite, with the value of *y*, the head and tail of *x*, respectively.

The danger of these operations arises because of the existence of common sub-lists, which may be forgotten by the programmer. If a list is changed and it is part of another list, then that list will also be changed. This sort of operation is often avoided, since at the end of a complicated piece of manipulation it may be difficult to remem-

20

ber the sources of lists. The power arises for two reasons. The first is the inverse of the difficulty. When a list is changed, all its uses change without any further work. The second is that it may remove the need to do a great deal of copying of lists.

Consider the problem of building up a list at the end instead of at the beginning. Since the end of the list has to be changed, we might have to copy the whole list with an alteration of the end element, if the end element could not be altered where it stands. A better alternative, if it were satisfactory, would be to build up the list in the other order and finally reverse it. But if it is being used while it is being constructed, this will not work. It can be done quite simply using *settl*. The name of the queue in the following program is *l*.

```
loop:x := nextatom;
if l = 0 then l := t := cons(x,0)
else begin settl(t,cons(x,0));
            t := tl(t)
      end;
```

4

MORE ADVANCED FEATURES

Each list processing language differs in the size of cell, the operations which are available and in the conventional representation of simple lists. It might seem best to allow freedom in these respects to the user, who could choose for himself the conventions most appropriate to his problem; but too much freedom has the disadvantage of machine code, and a settled and customary way of thought may be better than perpetual optimization and little communication. Languages do impose specific conventions, some of which are discussed and illustrated in this chapter.

If the restriction that each cell contains just two pointers is removed and suitable operations are introduced to examine the various parts of a cell, to create new cells and to alter existing ones, then the representation of objects within the computer becomes very flexible. It is not necessary to use the convention that the head pointer shows the items of a list and the tail pointer shows the next cell. Features of freer computer representations can be exactly reproduced on paper by the notation involving boxes and arrows. For example, the following might be the conventional representation of a straight list in some scheme.

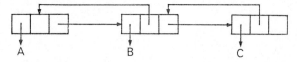

But when we write this list as

(A,B,C)

serious assumptions are made about the conventions. In the scheme above, such a list would be quite different in internal computer structure from the same list, written in the same way, in the conventions previously employed, where it would be

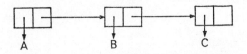

22

So the same simple notation can correspond to different machine representations in different list processing languages, and the operations provided will be quite different.

For example, the three-pointers-per-cell scheme given above is clearly intended to make movement about the list easily possible in both directions. This is not always easy in the previous representation. A trivial example of the utility of this can be seen from the following program. Suppose that a routine is to be written to find in a list of atoms, the atom which occurs immediately before a particular atom, x. In the structure with pointers in only one direction, a memory will have to be kept of the atom just before each atom on the list, in case it turns out to be the wanted one.

$$rep:a := hd\,(l)\,;$$
$$l := tl(l)\,;$$
$$\textbf{if } hd(l) \neq x \textbf{ then goto } rep\,;$$

In the structure with pointers in both directions the result can be found by moving back one place after the coincidence has been located.

$$rep:\textbf{if } first\,(l) \neq x \textbf{ then begin } l := down(l)\,; \textbf{ goto } rep \textbf{ end}\,;$$
$$a := first(up(l))\,;$$

Although the difference in this example is trivial, it would not be so if the coincidence had been established in quite another part of the program.

It is also possible to keep the number of pointers in each cell at two, but to change the conventions for the ending of lists. If recursion is not available and operations like *copy* are needed (which are awkward to program without recursion) then the spare pointer at the end of each sub-list can be used to indicate the place in the main list from which it is hanging (24). It is partly the provision of the memory of the place of return that makes the recursive program simple. It is necessary to indicate that the cell at the end of the sub-list is an end point and not merely a continuation of the sub-list, so some extra bits must be available for storing tag bits to imply this. When the procedure reaches a point in the list that is tagged as the end of a sub-list, attention is transferred to the place in the senior list from which it came, rather than going up one level in the recursion. This scheme has the serious disadvantage that a list can only be a sub-list of one list, and if it is needed as a part of another list then it has to be copied. Some problems suffer severely from shortage of store if common sub-lists are made impossible.

In this representation the list

(A,B,(C,D),E)

would be in the computer

23

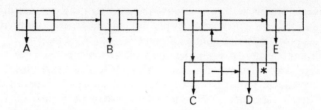

where the asterisk denotes the marker for the end of a sub-list. Note that the sub-list (C,D) points back to the place in the main list, and cannot therefore be a sub-list anywhere else.

Atoms

The representations of atoms in the computer is another feature where languages show considerable differences. Atoms are the pieces of information which are to be regarded as indivisible when a list is operated on. They might be numbers, or strings of characters representing the name by which something is known or perhaps information about it. The important fact is that their structure is not the concern of the particular program which is operating on the list in which they occur. They might consist of further lists, provided that some mark indicates to the system that they are atomic. An atom is not something which has no structure, it is something that is marked so that its structure is not considered as part of the structure of the lists which contain it. Provided that the system can distinguish it, a mark is enough.

Vectors

A particularly useful thing to be able to include in a list is a vector of information. By a vector is meant a set of stores which have consecutive machine addresses, so that the indexing operations of the computer are available to work on them and so that the possibility of calculating places in the table is present. The elements of the vector could be numbers, characters or more lists.

When a program requires access to the members of a list in an order which is not sequential (the easy order for lists), but is more or less random, say the fourth, twelfth and twentieth items of a list, then considerable inefficiency would arise from feeling along the list an item at a time in order to find the required elements. Instead, it is clearly better to make use of the facility which exists in all computers for retrieving items in terms of a base and a computed index. An advantage can also be gained in space economy. When quantities are organized in a complex way, with a lot of information in the structure, the fact that a large amount of store is taken up by pointers is no disadvantage. But when some of the data is easily used and represented in consecutive stores it is rather wasteful to use up perhaps half of the store expressing a very simple structure. The requirement for vectors can lead to considerable difficulties which will be discussed later. We give here some examples of its utility.

An obvious example is the ordinary vector of numbers. In this case it is likely that the computer will have orders which make taking the scalar product of two vectors an efficient process. This will depend on the vectors being stored in consecutive words.

A very important use of the vector of lists is in one of the methods of doing 'hash coding'. The problem is to find something which has been associated with an object, on being presented with the object itself. For example, it might be necessary to read the name of a man and find the information which has been stored about him. An attempt to do this by searching the list of all men's names would be impossibly slow if there were many men. This method of coding divides the average time taken by any predetermined multiple, n, the price being the space taken by a vector of size n. Instead of keeping one list of all men's names, n lists are kept, each of which holds approximately $1/n$ of the names. When a name is read, the appropriate list is selected and searched. If 26 is a suitable value for n and the unevenness of the distribution of initial letters is not thought to matter, then these could serve as the index for the lists. A vector of 26 lists could be kept and the correct one selected by an indexing operation when the name is read in. Since the index is a computed number, a vector is useful. Alternatively any function of the name could be used which lies in the range 1 to n and is fairly evenly distributed. A piece of program follows which will find the value associated with a name.

```
    l := read a name;
    i := function(l);
    x := listvector[i];
loop:if x ≠ 0 then
    begin y := hd(x);
          x := tl(x);
          if equal(hd(y),l) then
          begin value := hd(tl(y));
                goto exit
          end;
          goto loop
    end;
exit:
```

The difficulty that arises is that, if the best use is to be made of store at all times, then the vectors may have to be moved about in the computer, a process which is extremely slow and requires elaborate methods for updating references. This will be discussed in the section on garbage collection. It is possible to minimize the amount of shifting of data which has to be done by imposing some restrictions on the representations using vectors (3,6).

If the program is started with an area of store allocated for holding vectors, it is perfectly easy to continue to obtain new blocks until the area is full. By this time some of the vectors may have become unwanted. If new vectors are to be declared they can take the space from the unwanted areas, provided that they will fit in. If the blocks are not going to be moved about in order to accommodate new information, then neighbouring areas of unwanted store must be merged in order to offer the possibility of declaring large vectors. If the vectors are wanted for reasons of storage economy rather than to extract speed from the indexing operations it is possible to break the vectors up into pieces to fit in with the blocks of unused store available, provided that the separate section are chained together to indicate the structure. In this way an economy in the use of store is certainly achieved, since the proportion of pointers will never be more than in the case of one-item vectors, which would be what is provided by ordinary lists, and will in the starting phases of the program be very much less.

Circular Lists

It is possible to hold circular lists in the store of the computer and to represent them in the notation of boxes, though not directly in the notation of brackets. By a circular list is meant one in which a pointer in one of the cells indicates a place in the list from which the cell can be reached again. For example, the following lists are circular.

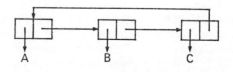

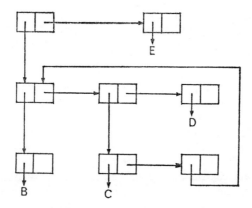

Such lists cannot be constructed using the procedure *cons* as the only way of forming new cells. For *cons* creates a list cell to hold two pointers to elements which were necessarily generated before the new cell, and cannot therefore point to it. Circularity can only be introduced by the procedures which alter an existing list. The statements

$$l := cons(a,0);$$
$$m := cons(c,cons(b,l));$$
$$settl(l,m);$$

create the list

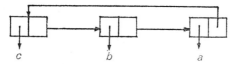

Circularity does not introduce any problems of programming, but it may have some effect on the system if it is allowed.

The bracket notation that has been used is not sufficient to express the nature of circular lists or the fact that a list can be a sub-list in more than one place. If we add the names of other lists to the items which can be written in lists, then we can express the precise structure. The third list above could be denoted

$$(x,E)$$
where $x = ((B),(C,x),D)$

Lists on Auxiliary Storage

When the store of the computer is too small for the problem or when results need storing for some time between runs, the lists may have to be put on backing store. The representation of a list on backing storage may be quite different from both the notation used in the computer and the notation used by the programmer. The computer's representation is unsatisfactory because, although it is a good form when the addresses given in the pointers are available, it creates considerable difficulties in reading the lists back into the store, since the same addresses cannot be used. Nor is the user's representation satisfactory, since it will often contain insufficient detail to enable the list to be regenerated exactly. For if a list containing common sub-lists is put on backing storage and then read down again, it will usually be necessary to create the same pattern of common sub-lists rather than just copying them out many times. Hence the detailed structure will have to be implicit in the backing store. However, the representation has the advantage that it is going to be read by the computer and not by a human, so it need not be humanly comprehensible. One possible notation is the one given above for circular lists, suitably compressed for machine use. The atoms also have to be represented in some way.

5

AN EXAMPLE OF LIST PROCESSING

In order to illustrate the use of list processing we shall consider the construction of a simple list program. This program will read a sentence and decide whether it corresponds with a set of grammatical rules which were read beforehand. The program is the basis of the method known as predictive analysis, which was devised by Kuno and Oettinger (33).

For this program we shall consider that the grammar of a language consists of a set of rules of grammar. Each rule defines one of the structures of a grammatical class, such as *noun-phrase, adjectival-clause* or *sentence*. For example, the following might be some of the rules which define the possible structures of the classes *noun-phrase* and *sentence*.

> *noun-phrase→the noun*
> *noun-phrase→the adjective noun*
> *noun-phrase→noun-phrase noun-phrase verb*
> *sentence→noun-phrase is adjective*

The name of the class is put on the left, and on the right is a list of words and class-names. The interpretation is that the right-hand side is an example of the class on the left. Using the second rule we might find that *the black cat* is an example of a *noun-phrase*, if we know that *black* is an example of an *adjective* and that *cat* is an example of a *noun*. Similarly *the man the black cat likes* can be seen to be a *noun-phrase*. The program is supposed to read a set of grammar rules of this form, and then to read sentences and attempt to decide whether they are properly formed.

The method of predictive analysis will work if in each rule the list of words and class-names begins with a word. The first two of the definitions given for *noun-phrase* would be satisfactory because they begin with the word *the*. The third would not be satisfactory because it begins with the class-name *noun-phrase*. It is possible to rewrite the rules for *noun-phrase* and make them comply with the restriction.

> *noun-phrase→the noun*
> *noun-phrase→the adjective noun*
> *noun-phrase→the noun noun-phrase verb*
> *noun-phrase→the adjective noun noun-phrase verb*

These rules will give exactly the same legal sentences. It can be shown that any grammar of this sort can be rewritten so that the correct sentences are legal and also the restriction is satisfied.

Let us assume that there is a list, consisting of words and class-names, which represents one of the possible structures of a sentence. We may assume that it starts with a word. A word of the sentence which is being checked is read and compared with the word at the front of the list. If they are different then this structure cannot correspond to the sentence. If they are the same then this is a possible analysis. The first word in the list has been checked, so it is discarded. If the second item is a word then we are in the same situation as before. Suppose that the second item is a class-name. Each of the rules which defines the class-name begins with a word. The next word of the sentence is read and compared with all these words. The rules which begin with this word may correspond with the structure of the sentence; the others cannot. From the original list we therefore construct several lists, one for each of the rules that began with the word that was read. Each of these new lists is formed by putting the remainder of one of the rules in front of the remainder of the original list. All these lists are then treated in parallel in the same way as the original one. If a list becomes empty, then an analysis has been found.

Consider an attempt to analyse the sentence *the man the black cat likes is ill*. The program starts with the four possible lists corresponding to *sentence* as defined above.

> *the noun is adjective*
> *the adjective noun is adjective*
> *the noun noun-phrase verb is adjective*
> *the adjective noun noun-phrase verb is adjective*

The first word of the sentence is read. Since it is *the* all the lists pass on to the next stage with the first word deleted. The next word *man* is a *noun* and so two of the lists are ruled out leaving

> *is adjective*
> *noun-phrase verb is adjective*

The next word deletes the list beginning with *is*. The other list begins with a class-name and so all the lists defining it are examined and their first words compared with the word *the*. This gives four possible structures for the rest of the sentence.

> *noun verb is adjective*
> *adjective noun verb is adjective*
> *noun noun-phrase verb is adjective*
> *adjective noun noun-phrase verb verb is adjective*

Continuing in this way, we shall find that the second of the above lists corresponds to the sentence.

This is a program suitable for list processing because its requirements for data space are unpredictable, because the structure of the grammar is important and because the use of common sub-lists can make a contribution to its economy. We shall assume that the rules for the grammar have already been read into the computer. Inside the computer the representation for the set of rules that defines all the possible structures for a particular class-name is a list of lists. The representation of noun-phrase would be

((THE,NOUN),(THE,ADJECTIVE,NOUN),(THE,NOUN,
NOUN-PHRASE,VERB),(THE,ADJECTIVE,NOUN,NOUN-
PHRASE,VERB))

Each of the items is either a word or a class name. If it is a word it is represented by an atom. If it is a class-name it is represented by the list which defines it. The class-name *noun-phrase* is represented by a pointer to the beginning of the whole list. This definition can give rise to circular lists, but it is a very convenient one for the program. The list called *t* is used to hold the set of possible structures. Those structures that are going to be compared with the next word are put into *l*. The process starts by putting into *t* the list of possible structures for a sentence and clearing *l*. The next word is read from the input by means of the procedure called *next word*, which we shall assume to have been defined. The program is given below.

The section between the label *loop* and the end is repeated for each word that is read. Each of the lists in *t* is put in turn into *s*. If the first item in *s* is an atom then it must be a word. If it is a word it has to be compared with the word just read, and if they are unequal then *s* is ignored. If they are equal then this is a possible analysis and the tail of *s* is added to *l*, unless the tail is empty in which case we have found a complete analysis. If the first item is not a word it must be the definition of a class-name. Each of the rules is placed in front of the rest of *s* and added to *t*. Note that we have to put a copy of the top level of the list in front of the rest of *s*. This can be done using the procedure *append*, which has the following recursive definition.

```
list procedure append(x,y) ; list x,y;
append := if x = 0 then y else cons(hd(x),append(tl(x),y)) ;
```

When the end of the conditional statement labelled *rl* is reached the list *l* contains all of the possible structures ready for the next word.

```
t := sentence;
loop:l := 0;   c := next word;
rl:if t ≠ 0 then
    begin s := hd(t) ;   t :=   tl(t) ;
        if atom(hd(s)) then
```

```
          begin if equal words(hd(s),c) then
                 begin if tl(s) = 0 then goto valid sentence;
                        l := cons(tl(s),l)
                 end
          end
          else
          begin u := hd(s);   s := tl(s);
             r2: if u ≠ 0 then
                 begin  t := cons(append(hd(u),s),t);
                        u :=tl (u);
                        goto r2
                 end
          end;
          goto rl
end;
if l = 0 then goto invalid sentence;
t := l;
goto loop;
```

6

GARBAGE COLLECTION

One of the most important features of a list processing system is the method by which it allocates the computer storage to the list structures. It would be very simple for the storage of the computer to be seized by the routines which need new space if it could be taken in a sequential fashion, cells being taken at the top of an area of free space and the top then moved up. But most list processing problems will require more store than can be made available in this straightforward manner, and something has to be done to enable the re-use of stores of which the contents are no longer needed. The economy of list processing depends on the ability to use space in such a flexible way that the store is occupied only by data which may be needed. All list processing languages provide, either explicitly in the language or implicitly in the system, some method of reclaiming store.

The very simplest method is that used by some 'real-time' programs and in other cases where the speed of reclamation is important and the structures simple. The storage which is to be used for lists is laid out before work starts in a single list called the free list. When a new store is wanted it is taken off the top of the free list and the free list pointer is moved down. When the user knows that he has finished with cells he informs the system which then adds them to the free list ready to be used again.

Suppose that the following is the initial free list. The word FREE indicates the top of the free list.

100	0,0	
101	0,100	
102	0,101	
103	0,102	
104	0,103	
105	0,104	
106	0,105	FREE

If the operations

$$cons(cons(cons(a,0),cons(b,0)),0)$$

are carried out, the store will contain

100	0,0	
101	0,100	
102	0,101	FREE
103	104,0	
104	106,105	
105	b,0	
106	a,0	

The first operation was to form *cons(a,0)*, the cell which was needed for this being taken from the top of the free list. The next operation was to form *cons(b,0)*, taking the cell from the new top of the free list. Cell 104 contains the result of forming the cons of 106 and 105, and 103 contains the answer. Now the free list starts in 102.

If the constituents of this list are returned to the free list in some arbitrary order, then the store might contain

100	0,0	
101	0,100	
102	0,101	
103	0,104	FREE
104	0,105	
105	0,106	
106	0,102	

So the free list soon becomes a tangle. This does not matter in the least, though it does mean that an attempt to understand how a program has gone wrong by printing out the contents of the store is usually impractical.

In a real-time system the cell size will normally be a few words. The store is laid out in a free list of blocks of this size, each block pointing to the next one. The blocks will contain numerical data as well as pointers.

For the simple scheme to work two criteria must be satisfied. The blocks of store must be of constant size and the user must be able to declare to the system that a particular cell will never be wanted again. Neither of these can be accepted as a wholly satisfactory restriction. The first is perhaps less difficult to put up with, since it is possible to make up cells of various sizes from lists of cells of one size. But the advantage of indexing within the block is lost and a considerable penalty must be paid in space to accommodate the pointers to link the cells together to form the block. Many list processing schemes do impose this restriction to one basic block size.

The second restriction is less easy in use. The system has to be told that a particular cell is not going to be used, rather than a particular list. If we write

$$l := cons(cons(a,b),0);$$
$$m := l;$$

34

and after some time decide that the list *l* is not going to be used any more, it is not possible to return the cells of which it consists if it will be used in its incarnation as *m*. We must be sure that a cell is not used in any list which may still be wanted, before it can be returned to the free list. Very much more difficult situations can arise in languages which permit the use of common sub-lists. If in the example above, *b* is a list and it is found at some time that *b* is not wanted, it must not be returned to the free list if it is still part of the lists *l* and *m* and either of these is wanted. This necessity for care can be a considerable difficulty to the programmer, who would really prefer not to know how his lists are made up and used in the computer. A convention, which has been adopted in order to make the memory of the wanted cells easier to the user, is to say that a list is owned in one place only. If it appears in other places it is being borrowed. The list that is the owner is responsible for declaring that the cells are not wanted.

The remainder of this chapter describes some of the ways of avoiding, in part or wholly, these two disadvantages of the simple and fast system, by paying with some combination of speed or other convenience.

The two main methods of avoiding the declaration of unwanted cells are to make the user declare either the unwanted lists or the wanted lists. In the first the user must still tell the system which lists are not wanted, but this will not imply that the cells of which they are composed can be returned to the free list until the system decides that all uses of the cells have been declared unwanted. In the second, the system decides which cells are on lists which it knows are wanted and therefore might be used, and which are not on any wanted list and so certainly can not be used. The latter can be put on the free list. The first system can operate gradually, the second tends to operate at specific moments because unwanted cells can only be detected by finding all wanted cells, and the process of determining these is quite slow. The first still requires the user to think about the unwanted lists; the second can be automatic (it is possible for the declaration of the wanted lists to be implicit).

Declaration of wanted Lists

When the system can no longer supply new cells from the free list, it must try to regain some of the space which is occupied by cells which will not be wanted again. The method described below is based on LISP. Any cells to which the user can refer must be on lists which depend from the known list heads, the definition of list heads being that they declare to the system all the active lists. A cell which is not referred to by an active list may be returned to the free list. But it is not possible to determine which are the cells not on the active lists except by finding all the cells which are on those lists and assuming that the others are unwanted. Hence the process of garbage collection has to proceed in two stages, the first of which goes through all the lists dependent on the list heads and marks them as wanted. The second then scans the whole area allotted to lists and returns the unmarked cells to the free list, simultaneously unmarking the marked cells ready for next time. Of course, if there are no unmarked cells the system has run out of store and the program must halt. Because the process of finding the wanted cells is fairly slow, since a large number of cells are usually on the wanted lists, it is best to do the garbage collection as infrequently as possible, when forced to by the lack of store.

The mark which indicates that a cell is wanted can be a bit of the word itself, or it can be in a separate store map: in either case the procedure for following the lists and marking them is as follows. For each pointer consider the cell to which it points, and if this has already been marked or if it is an atom, do nothing: otherwise mark it and then consider in the same way all of the pointers which it contains. This process is a typical recursive procedure.

```
begin integer j; list h;
    procedure follow list(l); list l;
        fl: if not atom(l) and not marked(l)
        then begin mark(l); follow(hd(l)); l := tl(l);
                        goto fl
                end;
    rl:if listheads ≠0 then
    begin h := hd(listheads); listheads := tl(listheads); goto rl end;
    freelist := 0;
    for j := 1 step 1 until listarea size do
    if marked(listarea[j])
    then unmark(listarea[j])
    else freelist := add to (freelist, listarea[j])
    end;
```

Because of the precaution of not examining lists which are already marked, the method works for circular lists without any trouble. Note that what is to be done about atoms is ignored in this discussion.

This algorithm has the disadvantage that, being recursive, it uses storage to remember its partial results. Because the amount of storage that will be needed cannot be foreseen and cannot be taken from the list area, difficulty may arise in providing this working space. An alternative algorithm exists which does not require the use of extra storage for garbage collection, but makes use of part of the cells which are being examined in order to hold the necessary memory of what is going on. It needs a number of markers to each cell which is equal to the number of pointers in each cell, instead of the single marker needed by the former system. It will be seen that

36

this program is rather similar to the iterative version of the program for copying lists, which could be done in this way if lists could be marked. The following program is for two pointers in each cell.

```
t :if not atom(l) and not marked(l,1) and not marked (l,2) then
begin mark(l,1);
      mem := hd(l);
      sethd(l,n);
      n := l;
      l := mem;
      goto t
end
else
s :if marked(n,1) and not
marked (n,2) then
      mem := tl(n);
      settl(n,hd(n));
      sethd(n,l);
      l := mem;
      goto t
end
else
if n = 0 then goto exit
else begin mem := tl(n);
           settl(n,l);
           l := n;
           n := mem;
           goto s
      end;
```

When a list is being followed, the memory that is needed is a pointer to the previous element. At a particular point in a list the variable n contains the pointer to the previous element and the variable l contains the pointer to the present element. If the cell is unmarked then it will be necessary to follow the list starting with the head of l, and hence l will be replaced by the value of $hd(l)$ and n by l. Since the value of the head of l is going to be remembered by l, the value of n which has been displaced can be remembered in the head of the cell l. Similarly when the head of a cell has been followed and the cell marked, the tail must be followed and the tail can be used to store the memory. The garbage collector can afford to mark and change cells, though ordinary programs cannot, because everything stops until garbage collection is finished.

This method is much slower than the simple recursive program but it can be resorted to if the simple program runs into storage problems.

An alternative way of obtaining store avoids the use of an actual list of free elements. When all the elements which are not wanted have been marked, no list of free cells is constructed. Instead an index is set to start at the bottom of the list area. When a new store is required, for example by the *cons* routine, a search is made from the point at which the index has stopped until a store marked as unwanted is found: this is then used. The index is stepped up so that the next store is taken from above. When the index reaches the top of the store a new process of identifying the unwanted elements is carried out. This method is neither less nor more efficient then the other, it merely redistributes the time used. For the time which was taken in forming the free list by searching the area for unwanted elements is now consumed bit by bit as new elements are needed. This partly removes one of the drawbacks of this group of methods, which is the need for a pause in time while the garbage collection is done. This is not embarrassing in a computer used in an off-line fashion, but when a computer is used on-line there may be a need to obtain storage space quickly at moments impossible to specify in advance. The existence of a pause while garbage collection occurs (which pause may well be of the order of one tenth of a second) rules out this sort of store grabbing.

It must be remembered that the system needs to know about all the heads of lists. Some of these can be declared to the system by the user, but some may be implicit in the program. For example

cons(cons(a,b),cons(c,d))

requires the *cons* routine to use three new cells. It may be evaluated in this order: first form *cons(a,b)* and remember it, then form *cons(c,d)* and finally form the result from these two. If there is room in the store to carry out the first of these but not the second then the garbage collector will operate when the second *cons* is called. The system must not collect the store used for *cons(a,b)*. In fact the partial result of the operation must be known to the system as a list head. This will apply not only to procedures like *cons* which are part of the library of the language, but also to the procedures which the programmer himself writes, the parameters of which may need to be declared to the system at moments when he is not in control. It is unfortunate that any omissions in the matter of protection from the garbage collector can be very difficult to diagnose.

If it is possible for the computer to know which quantities in its store represent numbers and which represent lists then the decision about which elements are list heads is capable of being made by the system. In that case, the programmer need not declare wanted lists. This automatic system can be very convenient. It could be done by some hardware device, keeping extra bits with each word in order to determine what sort of thing it is, but it will usually be achieved only by an interpretive scheme, which carries its own penalties in speed.

Declaration of unwanted Lists

Another method of garbage collection is used in the SLIP system, which is embedded in FORTRAN as a set of sub-routines (28). This scheme uses three pointers in each cell: one indicates an atom or a sub-list, one points down the list and the third points back to the previous member. With each set of items on a list are associated some further stores which are used for book-keeping. A list can be represented thus

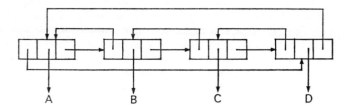

Since pointers go both ways in the list, each cell can be part of only one list. The book-keeping stores form the name of the list and all uses of this list point to them. Their function is to give access to both ends of the list and to count the number of references to it. When the list is made into a sub-list of another list, this count is automatically stepped up.

The store is organized into a free list. When the programmer decides that a list is not going to be used by him any more, he tells the system. The list is not necessarily made available as free space, but it is examined to see whether it is still wanted as a sub-list somewhere else, that is, whether the count of uses is zero. If the count is not zero, the list is still wanted, so it is not reclaimed but the count is decreased by one. If it is zero, then it is not in use anywhere else and its cells can be returned to the free list. The free list is attached to one end and the other end becomes the new free list. Since both ends are available through the control words, this can be done quickly.

This process has returned the unwanted cells, but the free list now contains pointers to lists which were once the sub-lists of the original list. It would be possible now to decrease their usage counts by one and return them to the free list if they are unwanted. But instead of doing this the lists are left hanging until the cells from which they hang are required. At this stage they are processed. This elegant method has the advantage that a certain amount of time is saved by not running though the unwanted list more than once, that garbage collection takes place just when the space is wanted and not unnecessarily, and that it proceeds gradually, throughout the operation of the program, and not in separate numbing bites.

Circular lists cannot be erased.

Garbage Collection and Vectors

The great difficulty about the use of blocks of store of variable size is that it may force the system to move information about in the computer, if the best use is to be made of space at all times. This can be a very slow and awkward process.

Suppose that the list area is initially blank, and that as new blocks of store are required they are taken from the top of the blank area. When this area is full and further blocks have to be accommodated, some use must be made of the storage which has been freed by blocks which are not wanted. The determination of the wanted and unwanted cells can be done by a process like either of the methods just described for constant block size. It is possible to know which blocks can be re-used, but while the area of usable store may be in total enough for the new blocks which are to be created, it may not consist of contiguous storage of sufficient size. If this is so, and if it is deemed unsatisfactory to abandon the programs which run into this trouble, then there is no substitute for moving about some of the pieces of wanted store so that the unwanted pieces are brought together.

Moving information is slow, indeed it is one of the reasons for introducing list processing that it avoids this sort of operation; it is a process which must take place in a single sweep and so puts the system out of action until it is complete, and it involves the up-dating of all the information which points to the blocks which have been moved.

A method which is not wholly satisfactory, but which minimizes the last mentioned disadvantage, is to have two areas of store, one of which accommodates the blocks of variable size and the other of which is organized in cells of unique size with a free list. If all references to blocks in the variable area are made through particular elements of the fixed size area, then the up-dating can be confined to single elements of that area. This offers no solution to the problem of the inefficiency of moving blocks.

7

SOME TYPICAL LIST LANGUAGES

IPL–V (21, 22, 23), LISP (17, 18), SLIP (28), FLPL (11) and COMIT (7, 31) are briefly discussed in this chapter. Further information can be found in the reference manuals and articles mentioned. A comparison of IPL, LISP, SLIP and COMIT has been made by Bobrow and Raphael (4) who include a tabular summary of their features.

For these languages the following questions will be answered where they are relevant.

1. What sort of structure does the language itself have? It may vary between something resembling machine code and an ordinary computer language like ALGOL or FORTRAN. This is very important to the user since it colours his thinking more than anything else.
2. How large a library of routines is available?
3. Are the primitive list operations available to the user?
4. Is the representation of lists fixed by the system, or has the user the ability to make up new representations?
5. What method of garbage collection is used and how much responsibility does it give the user? He may have to declare wanted or unwanted lists, and there may be other restrictions.
6. Is recursion easy?
7. How easy is it to do arithmetic? Is there a large library of ordinary numerical routines?
8. What are the standard notations for lists used by the programmer? Are there routines for reading and printing lists in a clear way?
9. Are there standard methods for representing lists on backing store?
10. How fast is the program produced?
11. Is an interpreter or a compiler used?
12. How are programs stored in the computer? They may be in the form of lists themselves, in which case it may be possible to modify programs or generate and obey new programs by the operation of the program itself.
13. Are common sub-lists allowed?
14. Are circular lists allowed?

IPL-V

The IPL-V system is an interpreter. It contains a master program which examines the user's program, one instruction at a time, and carries out the operations that it specifies. The hardware of the machine does not obey the instructions directly. The instructions are not held in consecutive locations in the store, but are themselves formed into lists, each of which is considered to be a sub-routine. The interpreter obeys in sequence the instructions which form a list, each of which might be one of the basic operations of the system or might name another sub-routine to be executed. Because the elements of the program are lists, they can be acted on by the program, so self-modification is possible.

The cells in IPL-V contain two pointers, as well as some further information which describes the pointers. The same format is used for data and for program. The two pointers indicate the item and the next cell in the list, and are called Symb and Link, respectively. The descriptive information is in two parts of the cell called P and Q. Numbers and characters are held in cells with particular values of P and Q.

The conventional paper description is different from any which has been mentioned in this book. Every list has a name and consists of a sequence of names. These names are either of other lists or of atoms. It is as if instead of writing

$$(A,B,((C,D),E,F),G)$$

we wrote

$$l = (A,B,x,G)$$
$$x = (y,E,F)$$
$$y = (C,D)$$

where each level is represented separately. This notation can give enough information about the structure in the machine to make clear the common sub-lists, without obscuring too much the form of the lists. In fact the notation differs in detail from the above. There are special conventions for making up the names which can be used. Names formed from a 9 followed by a number are local names, which are only significant within a particular list; names formed from a letter followed by a number are regional names, which can be used anywhere. A typical list might have the following appearance.

Name	PQ	Symb	Link
L2		9–3	
		9–1	
		G300	0
9–3		0	
		A1	

	V1	
	A2	0
9-1	0	
	S22	
	9-2	0
9-2	1	12

The name of the list which is being defined is in the name column. P and Q are empty for list elements. Symb shows the item of the list and Link is assumed to point to the next cell unless it is given. A value of zero for Link indicates the end of a list. The list called L2 has the items 9–1 (a locally defined list) and G300 (a regional quantity) on it. The local list 9–1 has S22 and the local quantity 9–2 on it. The value of 9–2 is the number 12. The function of the list 9–3 which is the first item in L2 is slightly different. Any list can have associated with it a description list which is stored as its first item. The description list of L2 is 9–3, the description list of 9–1 is empty. A description list consists of a number of pairs of attributes and values. For example, the value of the attribute 'Christian name' might be 'John'. Routines are provided for finding the value associated with a given attribute, for altering values and for adding and deleting pairs.

In instructions, the Symb part contains the name which is the argument of the instruction. The Q part of the cell tells how the Symb part is to be interpreted in order to evaluate a name, S. If Q is zero then S is Symb, if Q is one then S is the name in the cell whose name is Symb, and if Q is two then S is the name in the cell whose name is in the cell whose name is Symb. P specifies which of eight instructions is to be obeyed, according to the following table.

0 EXECUTE S.	S is the name of a primitive routine provided by the system or the name of one of the programmer's own routines.
1 INPUT S.	A copy of S is put on top of the push-down list called H0.
2 OUTPUT TO S.	The contents of the top of H0 is put into S and H0 is pulled up.
3 RESTORE S.	The push-down list of S is pulled up.
4 PRESERVE S.	A copy of the symbol in S is put on the push-down list of S.
5 REPLACE H0 BY S.	A copy of S is put into H0.
6 COPY H0 IN S.	A copy of H0 is put into S.
7 BRANCH TO S IF H5 IS —	If H5 is — then S names the cell to be interpreted next, if H5 is + then Link names the next cell.

The organization of IPL is based heavily on the use of push-down lists. The address of the cell holding the current instruction is held in H1. If the instruction specifies that a routine is to be performed then it is necessary to remember the place to return to after the routine is over. This is done by making H1 into a push-down list. Before the instruction transfers control to the named routine the present contents are pushed into the push-down list of H1. When the routine is finished the list is pulled up again into H1. This means that a routine can use itself recursively without trouble as far as the return point is concerned. A routine will normally need parameters. These are communicated to it by means of H0's push-down list. Each routine removes its parameters from H0 and leaves its results also in H0. A set of ten cells are provided for work space by any routine. These lists, W0 to W9, are safe, because every process which uses them must first push down their current contents and restore them after it has finished.

The IPL-V system contains about 150 basic processes. This is not a minimum set, but includes many operations which are frequently wanted. These routines are organised into eight classes.

1. General. Such operations as halt, set H5 to $+$.
2. Input-Output.
3. List. Such processes as insert a symbol on a list, copy a list.
4. Public working storage. For simplifying the use of the H0 list.
5. Description list processes.
6. Arithmetic operations.
7. Data prefix. These are operations to test the type of names.
8. Auxiliary storage. Operations to use backing store.

To handle repetitive processes a class of operations called generators is provided. These apply a specified process to each of a set of arguments.

The programmer is responsible for declaring that a list will not be wanted. When he does this it is then returned to the free list from which new cells are obtained. In order to enable him to keep track more easily of the lists which he wants, the lists are considered to belong to particular list structures, which have the right to erase them. Failure to erase lists results in a loss of storage.

LISP

The LISP system contains both a compiler and an interpreter. Programs produced by the compiler run between 10 and 100 times faster than the same programs under interpretation and use less space.

All the data are in a form referred to as S-expressions (symbolic expressions) which are represented on paper by the notation which has been used throughout this book. An atom is represented by means of a string of no more then thirty capital letters and digits, starting with a letter. Brackets and commas are used to indicate

44

structure though the commas can be left out. The two following S-expressions represent the same list.

((ROBINSON,JOHN),(SMITH,JOE))
((ROBINSON JOHN) (SMITH JOE))

The representation in the computer is in terms of cells containing two pointers. Although one of these is by convention kept to indicate the members of a list and the other to show the next element of the list, pointers to atoms can be put into either part. A special atom called NIL is used to signify the end of a list, but it can be used for other purposes.

Programs are written on paper in a form called M-expressions (meta expressions) which are translated into S-expressions by the programmer before insertion into the computer. The interpreter uses an internal representation of the program which is consistent with the format for data, so it is possible to write programs which modify themselves.

The form of a program is functional. It does not consist of set of instructions or statements to be obeyed in sequence, but it is a functional expression which is to be evaluated. For example, the following is an expression.

$$cons[cons[\text{A};\text{B}];\text{NIL}]$$

In order to construct interesting programs it is necessary for the programmer to be able to define functions for himself, to be able to express conditions and to have some way of repeating operations. Repetition is done by recursion, which is the main way of programming in LISP.

Conditional expressions are formed in the following way in the meta language.

$$[p_1 \rightarrow e_1; p_2 \rightarrow e_2; \ \ldots\ldots; \ p_n \rightarrow e_n]$$

Each p has the value true or false and each e is an expression which is a candidate for the value of the whole. The first p is evaluated, and if it has the value true, then the first e is the value of the whole expression. Otherwise the second p is evaluated and if it is true, the corresponding expression is used. If no p is true, the expression is undefined. The values of the e_i that correspond to p_i after the first true one are not found, nor are those of the e_i which correspond to false p_i. To define a function like *mem* which decides whether a particular atom occurs anywhere in a list, we use the recursive definition, identical in meaning with that in Chapter 3.

$$mem[a;l] = atom[l] \rightarrow eq[a;l]; mem[a;car[l]] \rightarrow T; T \rightarrow mem[a;cdr[l]]]$$

The value of the definition of *mem* is a conditional expression, with three p_i and three e_i. The functions *car* and *cdr* correspond to *hd* and *tl* (the names are derived from the names of parts of words in the IBM 709). The atom T stands for true. Note that one of the three p_i must evaluate to T, since the last one is T itself.

In fact, this notation is not used to indicate which variables in an expression are the parameters. The notation that is used is based on the λ-calculus of Church. Instead of writing the above definition for *mem*, we indicate the parameters *a* and *l* in the following way.

$$mem = \lambda[[a;l];[atom[l] \rightarrow eq[a;l];mem[a;car[l]] \rightarrow T;T \rightarrow mem[a;cdr[l]]]]$$

It is also necessary to indicate that the word *mem* in the definition is the same as the word *mem* being defined. A similar device is used, employing the word *label*. A proper definition of *mem* in the notation of M-expressions is

$$label[mem;\lambda[[a;l];[atom[l] \rightarrow eq[a;l];mem[a;car[l]] \rightarrow T;$$
$$T \rightarrow mem[a; cdr[l]]]]]$$

A large number of built-in functions are available to do commonly required operations as well as the primitive ones. These include some operations for doing arithmetic. Numbers are considered to be a special sort of atom, and they can be written in S-expressions.

Recursion is not the only method of repeating programs. When it becomes inconvenient or undesirable, a method of expressing a program as a sequence of statements is available.

If the programmer writes his program in M-expressions he must translate it into S-expressions before he runs it on the computer. The translation produces an awkward profusion of brackets and is not easy to read. The translation is defined as follows.

1. A function name, a variable name or an atom is written in upper-case letters.
2. A constant is translated into (QUOTE X).
3. The form f [*a;b; ... n*] is translated into (F A B ... N).
4. The conditional expression gives (COND (P1 E1) (P2 E2) ... (PN EN)).
5. λ[[*x;y;z*];*e*] translates into (LAMBDA (X Y Z) E).
6. *label* [*n;e*] translates into (LABEL N E).

The M-expression given above for *mem* translates into

(LABEL MEM (LAMBDA (A L) (COND ((ATOM L) (EQ A L)) ((MEM A (CAR L)) (QUOTE T)) ((QUOTE T) (MEM A (CDR L))))))

The functions which have been described are evaluated for the sake of their values, and do not change existing lists. Functions exist which change lists and are evaluated for the sake of their effects. The functions *rplaca[x;y]* and *rplacd[x;y]* correspond to what we have called *sethd(x,y)* and *settl(x,y)*. The names are derived from parts of the IBM 709 word.

Atoms are specially marked lists which are called property lists.

These consist of pairs of indicators and values. An example of an indicator is PNAME whose value is the printing name of the atom.

There is no provision for the use of auxiliary storage.

Garbage collection is automatic. The system knows all the heads of the wanted lists itself, since they are held in base registers which contain the list of all atomic symbols and in the registers containing partial results of computations and in other registers.

SLIP

SLIP consists of a set of routines embedded in FORTRAN. This means that all the power of FORTRAN to do arithmetic is available together with the very large number of existing programs. The list processing is not very fast even though this is a compiler and not an interpreter, because operations are provided by calling sub-routines and not by compiling sections of code into the program.

The FORTRAN input and output routines are available, and so is the FORTRAN use of backing store.

Program and data are quite distinct structures in SLIP and so there is no possibility of arranging for a program to modify itself. A large number of routines are available in the system, about 120 in some implementations.

The cells consist of two computer words in the IBM 7090, and they contain three items. Two of these are always pointers and indicate the next cell down the list and the next cell up it. The third item can be a number or it can be another pointer, this time one to the list element. Because the cells point both up and down the lists, any particular cell can only be in one list. But it is permissible for a sub-list to be a sub-list of many other lists. Every list has a header cell, by which it is known. All pointers to the list are really pointers to this header. It contains as its three items of information, two pointers, one to the top of the list and the other to the bottom, and a number which counts the number of times the list is used as a sub-list (for the purposes of the garbage collector). Every item on a list is either a number or a pointer to the header word of a list.

The primitive operations are available to the user. The most elementary are the following.

ID(CELL)	has as its value the identifier of the cell, which is a 2-bit field indicating the nature of the item.
LNKL(CELL)	has as its value the left pointer of the cell.
LNKR(CELL)	has as its value the right pointer of the cell.
SETDIR(I,L,R,CELL)	puts I into the identifier field, L in the left pointer and R in the right pointer of the cell CELL.

STRDIR(DATUM,CELL)	puts DATUM in the cell CELL.
CONT(A)	gives as its value the information in the cell whose machine address is A.
INHALT(A)	gives as its value the information in the word whose machine address is A.

Some of these operations have to be introduced to overcome the features of FORTRAN. For example, the two functions CONT and INHALT are used to avoid the fixed and floating point conventions.

The list called LAVS (list of available space) is used as a free list. The method of garbage collection was described in Chapter 6.

Circular lists can be created by the use of the primitive operations but they cannot be returned to the LAVS without the circularity being first removed.

Recursion can be done rather awkwardly, parameters and results have to be manipulated by the programmer.

FLPL

FLPL (FORTRAN list processing language) consists of a set of FORTRAN routines. The list structures resemble those of IPL. Each cell has two pointers or is a data word. Its nature is indicated by a description field of two bits. One of the pointers indicates the item, the other shows the next cell of the list. The method of garbage collection is for the user to indicate which are the unwanted cells. In order to help him to remember which cells are wanted, a bit is used in each cell to indicate that the item belongs to this list. If an item does not belong to a list then it should not be erased by that list.

Examples of routines are the following.

XCDRF(J)	has as its value one of the pointers of the word J.
XSTORDF(J,K)	puts one of the pointers of cell J equal to K.
XLASLCF(J)	finds the last cell on the list J.
XWORDF(J)	J is stored in a new cell removed from the free list.
XTOERAF(J)	erases the entire list J, including any sub-lists or data words which belong to J.

COMIT

COMIT is a very different type of language. The programmer is not required to think in terms of lists of the sort we have been discussing. The language was originally designed to help in the programming of research into mechanical translation. The language is very useful in a much wider variety of subjects, but it is specifically intended for processing information in the form of characters. The arithmetical facilities are poor. COMIT is an interpretive system.

The data for a program is in the work-space and in 'shelves'. Sophisticated operations are provided for examining the work-space to find sections of it which correspond to complex criteria, and for transforming the work-space. A fast method of dictionary search for items of information is automatically available.

The information is stored inside the computer in the form of lists of a conventional sort. All the control over which lists are wanted and which can be returned to free is done by the system and is inaccessible to the programmer.

The data consist of work-space expressions. These are sequences of items called work-space constituents. Each constituent can have some structure, but it is not possible for a work-space expression to be part of a work-space constituent. An example of a constituent is

ROBINSON / 23, SEX MALE, INTERESTS WINE WOMEN
SONG

Each constituent has one symbol, in this example the string ROBIN-SON, and a number of subscripts. One of the subscripts may be numerical and there may be any number of logical subscripts each of which may have further sub-subscripts. This is the limit of depth of structure of a work-space constituent.

A COMIT program consists of a set of rules. These specify how to locate and manipulate data, and how to find the next rule. A rule can have five parts, not all of which need be present in a particular example. It has a name by which it can be called by other rules in the program. It has a part which gives the name of the next rule. It has a left-half and a right-half which specify the searching and the operation, and it has a routing section which is concerned with input and output and the use of the shelves.

The left-half of an instruction specifies a search of the work-space. It consists of an expression similar to the expression that one wishes to find. The work-space is searched from left to right in order to find the first occurence of a match to this expression. But the expression given need not be an exact replica of the one wanted. For example, one could write only the symbol and the first item having that symbol would be found, no matter what its subscripts. Or a subscript could be given as well as the symbol and the first item to have at least the subscript and the symbol the same would be found. If we wrote

MAN / NAME SMITH

we might find an item

MAN / 23, NAME SMITH, INTERESTS WINE WOMEN SONG

A symbol exists in COMIT to stand for anything. A $1 means any single item. Thus

$1 / NAME ROBINSON

49

would ask for the first item in the work-space which has the subscript specified. The symbol $ in a left-half expression means find any number of things, so

$$A + \$ + B$$

means find the first occurence of A followed by any string of items followed by B. Searches can also be controlled by numerical values. One can ask for the first item with subscript greater than a certain number.

The expression written on the right-hand side is an instruction about what to do now that the left-half has been located. A constituent written in the right-half is inserted into the work-space. If the number n is written then the constituent of the work-space which matched the nth constituent of the left-half is copied into the work-space. Thus

$$A + \$1 + B = 2 + C$$

would find an item with symbol A followed by one item, followed by an item with symbol B. The A and the B will be deleted and a C inserted after the intermediate item.

Right-half expressions are available for using and altering subscripts and for numerical operations.

Backing store can be used in COMIT.

8

THE FUTURE OF LIST PROCESSING

List processing has proved itself to be a useful tool in compilers, in supervisor programs and in a range of symbol manipulation and non-numerical problems of a complex nature. It has most often been used by expert programmers or by people with problems which forced them to use it. If it were more easily and more widely available to the less expert programmer, it would probably be more used. Many programs contain sections which are suitable for list processing, for example the input of data in the form of words and the printing of variable messages. To achieve this wider use it is unlikely that special list processing languages will suffice. The ordinary user will not learn a special language unless it is important to his whole program: in any case it may be quite unsatisfactory for part of his work. List processing should be one of the many techniques at the disposal of programmers, for use in the part of programs which need it. It will be necessary to have a comprehensive language system which includes lists.

It is possible to see some of the features of such a language. Each of the existing languages has fixed on one or two of the methods of expressing programs. Each of these methods has some virtues, but for each there are problems which are more easily solved by the others. The language will have sequential orders as in assembly languages, FORTRAN and ALGOL; it will have functional definitions as in LISP and ALGOL; and it will have descriptive commands as in COMIT. For use by the inexpert the notation will have to be improved. In particular, the notation for the primitive operators is in many cases unclear, and complex uses of them are frequent. Consider a typical list expression in functional notation.

$$cons(a,cons(b,cons(c,cons(cons(cons(d,0),0),cons(f,0)))))$$

This is obscure. Arithmetic expressions avoid this by the use of infixed operators like plus and minus. A notation using the infixed operator comma makes the above expression quite understandable.

$$(a,b,c,((d)),f)$$

Another failing in list processing languages is the lack of good declarations. ALGOL has the ability to say that an identifier belongs to the real, integer or boolean class. The possibilities in list processing are much wider since the structure of the list can be described. It is very common to find that, when a new program is written, a great deal of effort goes into the choice of the representation of the objects. The programming does not begin until that choice has been made. The nature of most list processing languages forces that choice to be built into the program. Often, when the program is partly written, it can be seen that the representation chosen was not very satisfactory, and that a better one could have been used which would make the programming much easier or the program more efficient. The difficulty of changing the program can be so great that the inclination to do it is overcome, if the representation is built into every part of it. It is the aim of programming to separate out the features of programs which can be made logically independent, in order to clarify programs and make them easier to change. Accordingly, list processing would be easier if the user could, by means of declarations to the system, separate that part of his program which defines the structure of his information from that which defines the process.

Consider the following functional statement of an operation of even greater opacity than the previous one.

$$t := cons(hd(hd(tl(tl(l)))), cons(hd(tl(hd(tl(tl(l))))),$$
$$cons(cons(hd(l), cons(hd(tl(l)), 0)), 0)))$$

It is quite impossible to see what is going on here. But with a declaration of structure and the use of infixed operators the effect becomes plain.

> **list *l* with structure** *(a,b,(c,d))* ;
> $t := (c,d,(a,b))$

Not only is the program clear, it can be changed by altering only the structure declaration.

The natural tendency, which is well exemplified by current languages, is for each new language to include the best features of its predecessors, with a continual refinement of the way in which programs are written. We may expect that this will bring list processing into common and convenient use in the near future.

REFERENCES

Abbreviations: *CACM* Communications of the Association for Computing machinery

JACM Journal of the Association for Computing machinery.

1. Baeker, H. D. 'Mapped list structures.' *CACM*, Vol. 6, p. 435 (Aug. 1963).
2. Bailey, M. J., Barnett, M. P. and Burleson, P. B. 'Symbol manipulation in FORTRAN — SASP 1 routines.' *CACM*, Vol. 7, p. 339 (June 1964).
3. Berztiss, A. T. 'A note on the storage of strings.' *CACM*, Vol. 8, p. 512 (Aug. 1965).
4. Bobrow, D. G. and Raphael, B. 'A comparison of list processing languages.' *CACM*, Vol. 7, p. 231 (Apr. 1964).
5. Carr III, J. W. 'Recursive subscripting compilers and list-type memories.' *CACM*, Vol. 2, p. 4 (February. 1959).
6. Comfort, W. T. 'Multi-word list items.' *CACM*, Vol. 7, p. 357 (June 1964).
7. *COMIT Programmers reference manual*. MIT Press 1961.
8. Conway, R. W., Delfausse, J. J., Maxwell, W. L. and Walker, W. E. 'CLP — the Cornell list processor.' *CACM*, Vol. 8, p. 215 (Apr. 1965).
9. Evans, A., Perlis, A. J. and Van Voeran, H. 'The use of threaded lists in constructing a combined ALGOL and machine like assembly processor.' *CACM*, Vol. 4, p. 36 (Jan. 1961).
10. Fredkin, E. 'Trie memory.' *CACM*, Vol. 3, p. 490 (Sep. 1960).
11. Gelernter, H. 'A FORTRAN compiled list processing language.' *JACM*, Vol. 7, p. 87 (Apr. 1960).
12. Gelernter, H., Hansen, J. R. and Coveland, D. W. 'Empirical explorations of the geometry theorem machine.' *Proc. Western Joint Computer Conference*, p. 143 (May 1960).
13. Green, B. F. 'Computer languages for symbol manipulation.' *I.R.E. Trans.* HFE-2, p. 2 (Mar. 1961).
14. Iliffe, J. K. and Jodeit, J. G. 'A dynamic storage allocation scheme.' *Computer Journal*, Vol. 5, p. 200 (Oct. 1962).
15. Jenkins, D. P. 'List programming.' in *Introduction to system programming*. Academic Press, 1964.

16. McCarthy, J. 'Programs with commonsense.' *Proc. Symposium on the mechanization of thought processes.* N.P.L. HMSO, 1959.
17 McCarthy, J. 'Recursive functions of symbolic expressions and their computation by machine, Pt. 1.' *CACM*, Vol. 3, p. 184 (Apr. 1960).
18. McCarthy, J. *et al. LISP 1.5 Programmers manual.* MIT Press, 1962.
19. Newell, A. and Simon, H. A. 'The logic theory machine.' *I.R.E. Trans.* IT-2. p. 61 (Sep. 1956).
20. Newell, A., Shaw, J. C. and Simon, H. A.'Chess playing programs and the problem of complexity.' *IBM Journal of research and development.* Vol. 2, p. 320 (Oct. 1958).
21. Newell, A. *et al.* 'Information Processing Language V, Manual Sections I and II.' Rand Corp. P1918 (Mar. 1960).
22. Newell, A. and Tonge, F. 'An introduction to Information Processing Language V.' *CACM*, Vol. 3, p. 205 (Apr. 1960).
23. Newell, A. 'Documentation of IPL-V.' *CACM*, Vol. 6, p. 86 (Mar. 1963).
24. Perlis, A. J. and Thornton, C. 'Symbol manipulation by threaded lists.' *CACM*, Vol. 3, p. 195 (April 1960).
25. Research Lab. of Electronics and MIT computation center. *Introduction to COMIT programming.* MIT Press, 1961.
26. Shaw, J. C., Newell, A. and Simon, H. A. 'A command structure for complex information processing.' *Proc. Western Joint Computer Conference*, p. 119 (1958).
27. Weizenbaum, J. 'Knotted list structures.' *CACM*, Vol. 5, p. 161 (Mar. 1962).
28. Weizenbaum, J. 'Symmetric list processor.' *CACM*, Vol. 6, p. 524 (Sep. 1963).
29. Woodward, P. M. 'List processing' in *Advances in programming and non-numerical computation.* Pergamon, 1966.
30. Woodward, P. M. and Jenkins, D. P. 'Atoms and lists.' *Computer Journal*, Vol. 4, p. 47 (Apr. 1961).
31. Yngve, V. H. 'A programming language for mechanical translation.' *Mech. Translation*, Vol. 5, p. 25 (July 1958).
32. Yngve, V. H. 'COMIT.' *CACM*, Vol. 6, p. 83 (Mar. 1963).
33. Kuno, S. and Oettinger, A. 'Multiple path syntactic analyser' in *Information Processing 62.* North Holland, Amsterdam 1963.